On the cover: Cape Town skyline against Table Mountain

Third Edition, First Printing, 1997.

Library of Congress Cataloging-in-Publication Data

South Africa : a country study / Federal Research Division,
Library of Congress ; edited by Rita M. Byrnes. — 3d ed.
[Rev. ed.]
  p. cm. — (Area handbook series, ISSN 1057–5294)
(DA Pam ; 550–93)
  "Supersedes the 1981 edition of South Africa : a country study, edited by Harold D. Nelson."—T.p. verso.
  "Research completed May 1996."
  Includes bibliographical references (pp. 421–483) and index.
  ISBN 0–8444–0796–8 (alk. paper)
  1. South Africa. I. Byrnes, Rita M., 1943– . II. Library of Congress. Federal Research Division. III. Series. IV. Series: DA Pam ; 550–93.
DT1719.S67 1997   96–48983
968—dc21   CIP

Headquarters, Department of the Army
DA Pam 550–93

For sale by the Superintendent of Documents, U.S. Government Printing Office
Washington, D.C. 20402

South Africa
a country study

Federal Research Divisio
Library of Congre
Edited b
Rita M. Byrn
Research Complet
May 19

Foreword

This volume is one in a continuing series of books prepared by the Federal Research Division of the Library of Congress under the Country Studies/Area Handbook Program sponsored by the Department of the Army. The last two pages of this book list the other published studies.

Most books in the series deal with a particular foreign country, describing and analyzing its political, economic, social, and national security systems and institutions, and examining the interrelationships of those systems and the ways they are shaped by historical and cultural factors. Each study is written by a multidisciplinary team of social scientists. The authors seek to provide a basic understanding of the observed society, striving for a dynamic rather than a static portrayal. Particular attention is devoted to the people who make up the society, their origins, dominant beliefs and values, their common interests and the issues on which they are divided, the nature and extent of their involvement with national institutions, and their attitudes toward each other and toward their social system and political order.

The books represent the analysis of the authors and should not be construed as an expression of an official United States government position, policy, or decision. The authors have sought to adhere to accepted standards of scholarly objectivity. Corrections, additions, and suggestions for changes from readers will be welcomed for use in future editions.

Louis R. Mortimer
Chief
Federal Research Division
Library of Congress
Washington, DC 20540–4840